Joy Above Mental Clouds

A Practical Guide to Clarity, Peace and Purpose

Vishakha soni

Clever Fox® PUBLISHING

Chennai • Bangalore

CLEVER FOX PUBLISHING
Chennai, India

Published by CLEVER FOX PUBLISHING 2025

ISBN: 978-93-6707-211-0

Let's make our life
full of life

CONTENTS

Preface

Every book has its own story and its own timing to reach you, which is all unintended by the author before having an idea of writing a book.Similarly, this book was not intended to be written, but out of the blue, happened.

"Joy Above Mental Clouds" talks about the tough phases we all go through at certain points, where we get emotionally trapped in low feelings like depression, anger, frustration, distress, sorrow, fear, etc., and helps to realize how we are able to help ourselves to live a more fulfilling and happy life. This book is written in a very concise and straightforward manner. The language used in the book is very plain and easy to understand. This is a heart-to-heart talk to uplift us and other people who are still in the cage of their own thoughts.

"Joy Above Mental Clouds" book is not about teaching you spirituality or anything, just a basic conversation between us. To overcome negative emotions and help to analyze how you can develop a positive outlook on life. I mentioned here an overview of our root cause problems, to get a comprehensive understanding ofhow you can change it according to the situation or on any other aspect of life.

A few simple and effective techniques I mentioned in this book that helped me a lot to get out of my dark trap and you can use it too in your daily life, to overcome emotions that are not serving you for better, can put your life again in balance to live your life at its highest potential and would be able to make most of it.

The sole purpose of writing this book is to make you realize that you are not alone in this world, who is dealing with all this kind of stuff; there are many like you who are struggling and suffering in silence. There are many people around us who are fighting withemotions we never know about.

But you are one who decided to heal yourself and to live your life in a more positive and happy manner by picking up this book.

You can be a student, a parent, an employee, an adult, or anyone. Everyone wants to be happy. Right! But sometimes we can't figure out how to manage our emotions and get trapped. To make handling your emotions easy for you, I am here to help you.

Acknowledgement

I am not a professional psychologist or psychiatrist, but an ordinary person like you who wants to share my insights and knowledge on this sensitive matter that I gained through my emotional journey. I feel and think that there are more people who are still in the cage of their emotions and trapped in their emotional journey. To help by giving a direction of joy and stability to live purposefully and peacefully, through this book, I want to help you by providing insights and some personal experiences of emotions I felt, to make you know that you are not alone. I am here for you in the form of this book. Let's understand together these emotional problems and their solutions.

Let's get started!

Mental clouds

Imagine waking up in the morning and seeing dense clouds outside your window and feeling a relief from the sun's burning shine. Enjoying the scenic view from your room window. Then you turn on the TV and see the weather forecast that for the next few days the weather will be cloudy. Thunderstorms and hailstorms may occur. But you ignore it, because this time you are at peace with the weather. The next day, you again woke up, and saw the sky, filled with more dense clouds. Again next day, you woke up and saw the same view from your window, but this time you became a little bit disappointed. Then the next day, you see the same clouds. This time you become frustrated and as the days pass, the weather becomes more terrible with hailstorms and thunder storms, you can't see anything outside the window because of less visibility. Now, you are not enjoying the weather, you are feeling irritation, anxiety, and getting fearful and depressed.

I am referring to the negative emotions we all may have inside us as clouds such as fear, anxiety, anger, irritation, depression, pain, worthlessness, hopelessness, etc. These are our strong emotions that can take over our mind and trap our mind to get comfortable with these emotions and not live a happy life.

When a person consistently lives in the same emotion for a few days or weeks or months, or years, that emotional state becomes his/her state of mind. As we have seen in the example, how a most scenic view can take the form of a disaster when continues for a longer time. Let's delve deeper into this, to explore more about our emotions, feelings, and states of mind.

State of mind:

Consistent feelings are a state of mind we live in. It can be any feeling, positive or negative, all comes under one roof. Let's delve deeper. Let's take an example here –

You may know a friend or relative or any person who is always happy. No matter how opposite their life is going, how much struggle they are facing in everyday life which is often visible to everyone else. But they have an optimistic look at life. You may also know a person who is always full of negativity and negative thoughts inside their mind, always complaining, always blaming, always unhappy. You noticed!

I have one more example, two people met in a car accident against each other. They both have a dent in their car. One of them was blaming and yelling and demanding compensation for all losses, and the other one was trying to fix things. You see how two different people were behaving differently in the same situation.

How?

It is because of their different state of mind. One is in a calming, peaceful, and optimistic state of mind, while the other is in frustration. The person living in frustration was allegedly trapping himself in more negativity, maybe without even realizing. After this situation, he may find himself in other frustrating situations like being late for the office, spilling coffee over clothes, and it may become a chain of unwanted events. No matter what can happen, he will surely react in a negative way, only because of his state of mind.

You realize how we trap ourselves in negative situations just because we are not aware of our thought patterns and the emotions we carry.

Chain of thoughts:

Now, you may get a rough idea of your mental state. As we are already aware of the thought pattern,it is time to understand it in a more simple way. When we have a single thought in mind, it attracts more thoughts alike one after another. It all starts with one single thought, then another related thought, then another, and after a few minutes, it becomes a web of thoughts. It can be positive or negative, as per your thought pattern. You can check by paying some attention.

If it is positive, it is good. It will fill you with excitement and energy. But if not, then you may start to lose control over your thoughts and feel drained. For example, you are sitting in your office, working tirelessly, and one thought out of nowhere hits your mind, and it makes a chain of thoughts-

First thought - *"I don't like my job"*

Second thought – *"I don't like this work"*

Third thought – *"I am not paying well"*

Fourth thought – *"Ah man! I am not able to pay my bill this month,"*

You see how it started with one thought and made the person worried. Maybe you have more relatable examples. You can acknowledge. And for that, you have to delve deeper inside your thoughts and feelings.

Even when clouds grow thick The sun still pours its light earthwards

– Mark Nepo

Depression and Sadness

All of us are almost already familiar with the term. So I don't need to define it. Let's jump directly into the topic.

When I was in college, pursuing my Master's degree, I was clinically diagnosed with depression. Then I paid serious attention in this matter and came to know that there is a big misconception among people about depression and sadness. They are assuming it the same and calling sadness or depression one. I was doing it too, until I was diagnosed. But when I realized that depression is much more severe than sadness, I immediately got clicked.

Depression:

What does depression look like?

Depression is a severe chronic form of sadness for a long time.For instance, for days, for weeks, for months, for years, and some may have it for a lifetime. Not only mental, but there are many physical symptoms of depression too that can visibly notice. Some are listed here:

- *Over-thinking*
- *Feeling emotionally drained*
- *Difficulty in sleeping or insomnia*
- *Not able to enjoy things that one enjoys before*
- *Wanting to be alone*
- *Dark thoughts*
- *Negative self-talk*
- *Confusion in mind, like mixing of thoughts*

Now you may get a little bit clear understanding of what depression exactly looks like. If you can relate to any or most of these symptoms, hold on. If not, congratulations! Help someone else to figure out with the help of this book.

Sadness:

If we talk about sadness, it is just a low feeling we all feel at a regular basis in our daily life. It is a short-term emotion like anger, frustration, irritation, etc that lives with you for a short period of time, like for a few months, for hours, and then vanishes and you go back to normal.

You can understand the intensity of emotions with this example:

A lecturer walked around the classroom raising a glass of water and asking the students, how heavy is this glass of water? Answers called out ranged from 8 oz to 20 oz.

She replied, "The absolute weight doesn't matter. It depends on how long I hold it. If I hold it for a minute, it's not a problem. If I hold it for an hour, I'll have an ache in my arm. If I hold it for a day, my arm will feel numb and paralyzed. In each case, the weight of the glass doesn't change, but the longer I hold it, the heavier it becomes."

She continued, "The stresses and worries in life are like that glass of water." Remember to put than down in time.

Struggle in silence:

Many people struggle in silence with these worldly problems, making themselves feel like they are all alone in the world, dealing with sadness and depression. It may seem normal to other people around them. But only they know how badly it is affecting their daily life. They know this feeling. If you are one of them, then you may also know this feeling.

If people dealing with depression and sadness try to talk to any of their close ones, like friends, family, etc., people can't actually understand the depth of feeling, and try to help us as per their own understanding of the intensity of emotions. But they actually cannot reach that depth, and this feeling leads to the birth of loneliness, where we isolate ourselves and just try to survive.

Surviving with these high-intensity emotions is very difficult. But we still try to cope with this, because there is always some hope in the corner of our heart that says out loud to us that "It will be all ok one day". It is our soul talking to us. Some people just neglect this voice and remain indulged in those feelings. But some of us are brave-hearted, who believe and know that they are going to defeat it.

Mind-body connection:

Our thoughts inmind and our physical body are directly connected, or interconnected with each other. When we have any positive or negative thought in our mind, our body reacts to it directly or indirectly.

Imagine you are going on a romantic date. You imagine how it would feel, or a single thought of your love makes you feel tense in your solar plexus, you get nervous. Your body can feel.

That's how it relates to our body.Similarlythere are negative impacts on our bodytoo when we have negative thoughts in our mind.

When we feel tense for a long time, our immune system gets weakened and negatively impacts our body.

Rewiring of the mind

Rewiring of the mind is a powerful mental process that happens throughout our life. Let's understand it scientifically, it is the brain's ability to organize or reorganize itself by forming new neural networks and connections.

For example, let's say you want to learn to play guitar. You are a beginner. So you start with an easy chord and string rhythm patterns. After a few weeks, you become better and after a few months, you play like a pro. How did it happen? It happened because of the formation of new neural networks and connections in your brain.

When you do or think somethingconsistenly, it becomes a pattern, and how we feel becomes our state of mind, which is scientifically termed as "neuroplasticity".

Understanding negative thought patterns:

When we consciously keep an eye on our thoughts. We can notice that most of our thoughts are negative. It is not a surprising thing because it is our habitual ways of thinking that reinforce negative emotions and behavior.

Let's say you are in a job, you get a promotion. Now your responsibilities have doubled and you feel more stressed and frustrated about the workload. You consistently feel this stress in every single cell. The more you feel, the more your mind fills with negative thoughts and viceversa. Is there nothing positive in the new role, like increment, power, a team under you, etc.?There may be a number of things you won't like, but there are positives too. Isn't it? Then why are you seeing only negative ones? Because your brain is wired to complain. You realize it or not, it unconsciously became your thought process. Admit it.

Recognize patterns:

It is crucial to recognize and understand these patterns to change them. To recognize it, we must have to be conscious of our thoughts and feelings. The more you pay attention to your thoughts and feelings, the more you will have control over them. The more you become conscious of it, the lesser energy it will have to respond.

I am not saying that feeling negative emotions is a sin. We are humans, and we get it as our natural thing from birth to feel positive as well as negative emotions. It is ok to feel anger, irritation, disappointment, and restlessness. They are not bad. Don't suppress. If you suppress, it will take a more dangerous form inside you unknowingly.

But then, what to do? How to deal with it? Just let them flow. Yes. When you feel negative emotions without indulging yourmind in judgemental state, it will release. Don't be harsh and don't suppress. Accept them, but don't nurture them.

Habits of the brain:

Our brain is like a stubborn kid. It is a tough task to control it, but once you get a technique, you win the battle. But how to handle it? There are a number of tricks our brain plays to make us stay in those negative emotions, here are some:

- ***Catastrophizing***: Catastrophizing is the brain habit of imagining the worst possible outcome in any given situation. This can lead to increased feelings of fear and anxiety. For example, a person who makes a minor mistake at work imagining that they will likely be fired.

- ***Overgeneralization***: Drawing broad, negative conclusions based on a single event or limited evidence. It can create a negative outlook on life can reinforce feelings of failure. For example, failing one exam leads to the belief that one is useless or a failure in all areas of life.
- ***Black and white thinking***: All –or –nothing is a viewing situation in extremes, without recognizing the middle ground. This creates unrealistic standards and contributes to feelings of inadequacy, lack, and failure. For example, thinking you're either a complete success or a total failure.
- ***Mental filtering***: Focusing exclusively on negative aspects and ignoring any positives. Leads to persistent dissatisfaction and a negative view of personal experiences. For example, remembering only the negative feedback from a performance review, despite receiving praise as well.
- ***Disqualifying the positive***: Rejecting positive experiences by insisting they "don't count". Reinforces negative self-perceptions and prevents positive reinforcement. Receiving a compliment on your work, but believing the person didn't really mean it. They are lying.
- ***Jumping to conclusions***: Assuming that others are thinking negatively about you. Predicting that things will turn out badly. These assumptions can create a

self-fulfilling prophecy and contribute to anxiety and depression.

- ***Emotional reasoning***: Believing that negative emotions reflect reality. It can lead to a distorted view of the world and oneself. Thinking like "I feel worthless, therefore I must be worthless."
- ***Should statements***: Having rigid rules that you and others should follow and feeling angry or guilty when these rules are broken. These statements can lead to feelings of frustration and inadequacy when expectations are not met. Thinking "I should always be perfect" or "I should never make mistakes".
- ***Labeling and mislabeling***: Assigning labels to yourself or others based on a single instance. Labels can perpetuate judgements, reinforcing depressive thoughts. Calling yourself "a failure" after a minor setback.
- ***Personalization***: Blaming yourself for events outside your control or believing you are the cause of external events. Leads to unnecessary guilt and self-blame. For example, believing your friend's bad mood is because of something you did.

What we sow
we reap

Memories

Every day we make a lot of memories. Our mind is filled with infinite memories. Happy memories, sad memories, good memories, bad memories, depressed memories, exciting memories, traumatic memories, and a lot more like these, which give us the exact emotional feeling of that particular event of our life.

For example, in your childhood, you went to a restaurant. The smell of that restaurant was really good. You ordered your favorite coffee. It smelled really strong and good. You, without realizing, were experiencing it all in the present moment. And it gets stronger with every breath. You enjoyed it a lot. After a few years, you went to a café in a different city and the same smell of coffee triggered you. You remembered that specific smell of that particular restaurant.

Memories play a significant role in our daily lives. It makes us feel more lively every day. It helps us in our numerous task and chores to perform well. It also plays a role in shaping our emotional, mental, and psychological states when it comes to emotional disasters such as depression. Both positive and negative memories can influence the severity and persistence of depressive symptoms.

Positive memories give us the feeling of that pleasant time when we were actually happy, and negative feelings make it severe to feel. Here, we will specifically talk about the negative memories. How does it impact our mental health and other aspects of it?

Negative memory:

We all had a number of memories stored in our brain. Some of them may be negative, like embarrassment, insult, ignorance, a loved one, failure, a person, and maybe of anything. Memories give us a strong flashback of past events, may be of those that were not so fruitful and are definitely not worth remembering. But our stubborn mind gives us the repeated flashbacks of memories we want to forget. Ever happened to you? That after a particular event you tried to forget it, and the more you tried, the more it became a clear image in your mind.

Why? Because your whole attention unconsciously was on that particular memory, you were consistently giving the vital energy to the memory to get a strong hold in your mind, and the emotions that memory holds started to take over your whole bodily emotions.

A good example of this is parting ways with your loved one or a break-up. That breaks you down. You cannot get over that person. Your mind is recalling all the beautiful memories you made together. Your romantic dates, anniversaries, adventure rides, star gazing, phone calling, etc., all are coming in front of your eyes day and night. You try to forget him/her, but fail.

> *"We suffer more in our imagination than in reality"*
>
> **– Seneca**

Persistence and recalling:

Depressed individuals tend to recall negative memories more frequently and vividly due to the brain's negativity bias.

There are many neurobiological factors that give shape to our memories to feel sad and depressed. Let's understand scientifically, the 'amygdala', a small part of the brain, that is responsible for releasing emotions, links our brain to memories.

So, when our past negative memories take the forefront of the brain, we feel depressed. The Amygdala is more active during stressful or traumatic events, strengthening the memory of the experience.

Along with memories, our brain habits make it more severe and pervasive. As we already learnt in the last chapter, about the brain's tendency to be habitual with one thinking pattern. For example, catastrophizing, over-generalizing, labeling and unlabeling, black and white thinking, etc.

Why do negative memories have more potential to be recalled than the positive ones?

Negative memories are more vivid and easier to recall than positive ones due to their heightened emotional content. When we feel happy, we feel free, our heart expands, brain relaxes. But when we feel negative emotions, our muscles contract, as a result, we feel drained, that holds a more strong effect on our mood and behavior, leading to prolonged periods of sadness and anxiety.

Memories can
never be erased,
it will always
add on

Emotions

From a scientific aspect, emotions are nothing but energy in motion, which we feel inside our body and release through our body in the outer environment.

But in human form, emotions color our world. Influence our thoughts, actions, and interactions. It is like waves of the sea touching the sand of the beach. They are the compass that guides us through life's journey. They make us feel alive within our body, giving us a sense of being.

There are many types of emotions we feel, like positive, negative, and sometimes mixed. Where positives give us meaning to be alive, there are negatives too that obscure our paths. Understanding our emotions is a crucial step towards navigating through the mental fog and discovering the joy that lies above.

> *"Emotion gives us oneness that holds us together."*

No doubt we all feel the same emotions in similar types of situations, but the intensity of feeling emotions may vary from person to person. Some feel emotions at the surface level, some at the intermediate and some at the core of their heart.

Those who feel emotions at the depths of hearts are more likely to be depressed by small things and happy at the same time. But this is not a thing to be ashamed of. Actually, this is a strength.

Nature of emotions:

There are usually two types of emotions we feel, which separate our consciousness from one event to another

*Basic emotions***:**

Basic emotions are emotions that we feel in a straightforward way. Happiness, sadness, anger, fear, surprise, disgust, etc. are some emotions that come under the basic category that we often feel.

*Complex emotions***:**

Emotions arise from combinations of basic emotions such as guilt, shame, pride, and love. This is a mild mix of emotions, where we feel a lot of emotions at the same time. A good example is *love,* in which we feel pure happiness, nervousness, security, and anxiety at the same time.

How do emotions manifest physically?

Let's understand with an example, when you encounter a snake, your body's immediate response triggers physiological reactions, such as a spike in heart rate and rapid breathing, to prepare you for a 'fight or flight' response.

Similarly when we are in tension and depression, our body responds in different ways and obviously in a negative way. That's how our mind and body connect physiologically.

Techniques to reframe:

- ***Self reflection***: Be more aware about your emotions; the more you will pay attention to your emotions, the more you have the control over it.
- ***Journaling:***Do journaling in your spare time. Take a diary and start to write your emotional structure like

events, conversation, etc. It will give you a check on your own emotions.

- ***Grounding exercise:*** Engage the five senses to bring awareness to the present moment. Be more aware of what you see, hear, smell, feel, taste.

Emotion gives
us oneness
that holds us
together

Self-talk

Self talk refers to the internal dialogue we have with ourselves, encompassing our thoughts, beliefs and reactions to various experiences.

We all do self-talk in some manner at many times a day, while thinking, while driving, while making decisions, while adoring ourselves, while working.

We know our true emotion at deepest. So we talk honestly with our self. At least we don't need to fake anything with ourselves. So we share happiness, excitement, anger, guilt, frustration, hatred, with our self in true form.

We love to do it, because when we do self talk, we often tell ourselves the things that we deeply desire to listen or feel.

Although it is highly exciting thing, but we often misuse it a lot by negative self talk that harms us internally.

Let's understand how positive and negative self-talk influence our thoughts, emotions and behavior.

Positive self-talk involves encouraging, supportive, and affirmative thoughts that promote self-confidence and high self-esteem. For example:

"I am capable of overcoming challenges."

"I can do it."

"I have difficulties and now I am a stronger person than ever before."

"I deserve happiness and success."

On the other side, negative self talk is characterized by critical, self-harming thoughts that undermine confidence and self-esteem. For example:

"I am not good enough"

"This will end in disaster"

"I don't deserve any live and respect from anyone"

"I am a failure"

It is really important to check what you are feeding your mind. How you are communicating to yourself at daily basis. We can lie to other person, but we can't do to our self for a long time.

Exercise:

Here are some techniques that helped me and can help you too to change it for better:

- ***Self-awareness:***Pay attention to yourself-talk, it will give you a comprehensive understanding of your own self-talk pattern. Once you get where you are lacking, then only you can change it
- ***Self- talk check in:***At the end of each day, before sleeping, reflect back on moments of self talk and categorize then as positive or negative.
- ***Ask questions:***Ask questions to yourself that what I am thinking? And what I am going to say now? It will give you chance to rethink your thoughts that are going to communicate with yourself.
- ***Affirmations note:***Say positive affirmations to you to reframe yours thoughts, to build new neural connections. You can paste it too where ever you want, from where you can easily see it and affirm it, like on

office desk, your car, your fridge, anywhere you can easily see.

- ***Positive self talk:*** Talk positively to yourself. Accept your flaws. Embrace yourself.

The things we say to ourselves hold the highest impact on our self- esteem and confidence rather than others

Blame game

Blame game is the act of attributing responsibility for negative circumstances or problems to others instead of confronting one's own role and behavior.

This happens when we feel insecurity inside us, when we try to avoid feeling guilt or fear of accepting or confrontation and try to back out.

Blame game is a common habit that many of us fall into. It provides a temporary glass shield against the discomfort of facing our own shortcomings or the realities of a challenging situation.

External blaming:

We fear taking responsibility for our own actions or simply neglect it by saying that I didn't do anything. And the easiest way we find to get out of the situation is by blaming the other.

When we blame others, we create a barrier to personal accountability and remain trapped in a cycle of negativity.

This not only affects our emotional well-being but also erodes our connection with others. For example:

"A man who struggled with anxiety and was quick to blame his friends for not understanding him"

Self-blame:

We don't always blame others. It can be vice-versa. Sometimes we blame ourselves for mistakes we perform in past and present as well or any circumstance we faced that involves us in some way. We take the whole responsibility of that events, fill our self with guilt and shame, leads to negative emotions like anxiety, depression.

Self blame can feel like carrying a heavy backpack filled with stones – each negative thought and belief make us down, make it difficult to move on.

Self-criticism:

Many of us develop this inner critic, shaped by our experiences with authority figures and societal expectations. It becomes a learned behavior, convincing us that we must strive for perfection to be worthy. We often self criticize us by saying things like:

"I failed because I am not good enough, I will never get it right"

"It all happened because of me, I must get punished"

Practical exercise:

- ***Questions to consider:***When did you last time blamed anyone for your mistakes? How were you feeling? Observe past events and remember the feeling you felt. Was that feeling and action worthy?
- ***Communication:***Making mistake is common. Try to communicate and confront things in easy way. Communication can be a key to resolve this habit.
- ***Don't take charge of everything:***Take note of things that you can control and that you cannot. Don't try to control everything.
- ***Forgive yourself:***Don't hold negative emotions for too long. Just admit and forgive. Learn to move on.

> "When we feel good about choices we are making and when we are engaging in the world from a place of worthiness rather than scarcity, we feel no need to judge and attack"
>
> – **Brene brown**

Emotional Dependency

We already discussed emotions. But what does it mean of emotional dependency? It means that sometimes we become too much emotionally dependent on others more than we need. It can be happen because of various reasons like feeling of insecurity, fear of loneliness, etc.

It is not a sin to depend on others with respect to our emotions. We are humans and humansare social animals. No doubt we need people in our life to communicate, to live with, to hang out and to share our problems and grief. But as long as we don't try to control our emotions, we become depend on others. We start to please them to stay, whether they want, or not.

It creates an over-possessive and over protective nature within us. That is not so good for relations. I know many people come under category of over sensitive people. They may be over loving, over nurturing, but a need of space is always present, doesn't matter what the relation is.

Chase people:

Iknow a friend of mine who was single in status after many failed relationships. She was looking for a partner from a long time. And when she finally met him, she easily fell in love with him. She loves him, she cares for him, she treats him like he is the only world for her. She called him day and night. Always asking questions about his well-being. She was doing more than enough for him. But this relationship failed. You know why? Because of over-chasing in love. Her partner got frustrated because of her over-protectiveness and over-possessiveness. He loved her too, but there was no room for individual privacy and he cannot even breathe freely.

Maybe you saw some examples like this around you. It is good to provide love and care. It is good to nurture. But everything is harmful in excess.

Healthy boundaries:

When we fail to set boundaries, we may feel overwhelmed, constantly giving to others while neglecting our own needs. Conversely, healthy boundaries allow us to honor our own feelings and maintain balance in our interactions.

Healthy boundaries are like protective fence around a garden – allowing sunlight to enter while keeping out weeds that threaten to overtake the blooms. Establishing healthy boundary is essential for maintaining emotional balance, personal space, and self-respect as you can see in above example.

Meet your inner self:

Whether we admit it or not, we all live individual lives at the core. It is not always important, and may not always be possible to have someone around you to support your emotions.

Life is a journey, and it has a lot of good and bad circumstances in its stock for us. And everyone's journey is different. Even your siblings don't live the same life that you are living. There might be situations where you might not find people to provide assurance whenever you feel overwhelmed in irrelevant situations. No. Sometimes you will find yourself alone in great need of someone else to support you. But you have to be with yourself.

Did you ever notice? When you desperately want to talk to someone, you find them busy. It happens. It feels very uncomfortable. Right! Everything is uncomfortable at first. When you get used it, it seems better. And sometimes, you have no option other than staying with yourself.

Befriend yourself:

The most loyal and always available friend I found on earth is me to myself, who always listens to me, guides me, lovesme, takes care of me, nurtures me, who knows my deepest needs and desire, always ready to take a stand for me, who knows mebetter than any other person can on earth.

Isn't it beautiful?

It's amazing, I will say.

Having a lot of friends outside is a beautiful feeling. But becoming your own friend hits different. Some of you may already be familiar with this feeling. How great it feels when you no longer need someone, or you interact with people just for fun. Your circle expands, your relations improve. You have a feeling of fulfillment and satisfaction within you that is no longer overwhelming you.

"The most important relationship in the world is the relationship you have with yourself. Because it doesn't matter what happens, you will always be there for you."

– Diane Von Furstenberg

To be free, one must overcome dependency

How life works

Life has its own philosophy. It has its own happiness and sadness, challenges and peace, love and hate, wins and defeats, truth and lies, sour and sweet. It is a mash-up of everything you can name.

It is a multifaceted lesson for us that we need to learn lifelong, till our last breath. Every single person here has a different life, with different experiences, with different phases in different faces at different times to make us learn different lessons that are necessary for our personal growth and satisfaction with life.

But why are these lessons sometimes extremely painful?

Let's understand, when we were studying in first grade, the level of study was not easy for us at that time. Right! Then we moved to second grade, which was even harder than the first. Then we moved to third, then fourth, then fifth........and then where we are today. If I ask you whether youcan teach a student in first grade now, you will say with a lot of confidence –

YES! I can teach.

This is the same class you found hard at one point. Remember!

Similarly, life works in the same way. It shows us what we found difficult to deal with, to teach a lesson that we never knew we needed. To make us personally grow.

When we do a thing we fear most, confidence generate inside us. We become ready and excited to pass the next, just like the above example. It is utmost important for us to deal with our fear. Most of the time, fear is the main reason that blocks our life from living it joyfully and peacefully.

Life has a lot of lessons for us in its store, that's why it is so unpredictable. We can never be sure what can happen next. Everyone is living a different life; you cannot compare your life with anyone. We can never know everything about the lives of other people.

Maybe you faced some difficult challenges in your life. That made you extremely disappointed. You started questioning yourself –

Why me?

Why all this happened to me?

Because you have not yet learn the lesson life wants to. Sit comfortably, analyze the situation you are in, and try to figure out what is good in it? If you ask, you will be guaranteedto get the answers.Answers can be shown to you in any form, maybe in a scene of a movie you watch, strangers talking next to you say a line that immediately clicks with you. Just ask! You will get the answer at the right time.

But you have to analyze it on your own. No one else can do it for you. When you will begin to look for good things in challenges, you will discover a path to come out of these clouds and will have mental clarity more than ever before you are seeking right now.

I was in this situation for many years. But now, when I look back on my life, it all makes sense now.

> "Things don't come to us when we desire;they come when it is the right time. Until then, we have to figure it out on our own."

What we see, we believe. What we believe, we perceive

Everything is connected

Life is like a film script. It already knows what we will need at what time, which we are totally unaware of. Every single circumstance and event in our life happens based on this particular theory.

When life puts us in a situation where we are clueless about what is happening? Why it is happening? Why only me? How is it happening? We are on a journey of something valuable and insightful. Every lesson we learn in our lives has a background work which we never observe. We just see the superficiality of things and perceive or judge them as they appear to us currently.

But no!

It is way more important than that. Just remind a moment, whenever you learn something valuable from your challenge and made perceptions on it. Now, go a little bit into more detail. What small circumstances happened to you that led you to reach this lesson to make you realize that lesson?

Life doesn't work in an arbitrary way. Nothing happens to us without meaning. Every single event we conquer or face takes us on a step ahead that we never knew before, and it makes everything possible effortlessly if it's meant to be. If it is right for you, otherwise, you will learn a lesson and will try an alternative, which will itself prove even better than before. It will show you why things never worked before. You will consider things in a more positive way.

But to reach this analysis, you have to do a little bit of hard work. You have to consistently observe things in a more mindful and optimistic manner, and will have to go to the depth of things, beneath the surface.

Intuition:

Intuition, which we commonly call "gut feeling", is a powerful voice exists in all of us inside our hearts. I don't know what exactly it is, some call it god, some call it divine power, some call it an angel, and some call it spirit guide. I call it the higher self, who knows everything about my life, my past, present, and future. Everything!

My higher self guides me in every single step, making my life more purposeful and meaningful. And the best example I have to share is this book you are holding in your hands or perhaps seeing on your screen.

I never knew I would be drawn to write a book. I never write anything before. In my difficult time, when I was feeling very lonely. And was feeling helpless from every direction. I took support from self-help books. I was reading book one after one to understand the situations in more wider perspective and was seeking help to get out of it. And now, I am here, as an author of this book, trying to help you with the same. When I look back, it all makes sense now. I trusted my intuitions over anyone else.

Everybody has this divine gift of intuition, but most of us neglect it most of the time because our analytical mind interrupts in between, giving us every possible reason not to listen to it.

But when we rewire our brain, as we earlier learnt, we tend to become more mindful and intuitive at the same time by honestly listening to our intuitions, which responds to us really well than anyone.

The more you listen, the more it will guide you. You don't need to take a step directly to the climax part in one go. Just take little steps daily. Be more attentive to your inner voice and follow it when you find any need to question it.

Trust it!

Unfolding life:

Life is a layered and multifaceted thing. When we give some access to life to play itself, without trying to control it very hard, it unfolds its deepest hidden secrets in front of our eyes, and we wonder.

I know this is sounding a little bit philosophical. But this is true. I am living this truth. We are not separate from the universe. We are part of it. We are nature. Everything that already exists in the universe is accurately at its defined perfect place where it needs to be.

You can see it everywhere, in the bark of trees under a microscope, body anatomy, and the distance of the sun from the earth. Everything is connected, you and me too, where we need to be.

Life unfolds itself, When we surrender

Inner world and outer world

We talked about the world and worldly things. Now we can go a little bit in more detail to know what the world actually means to us?

From the very first chapter, we are discussing mind things and worldly things separately. Now, it's time to put two different worlds in one frame.

When I say world, what thought or image comes first to your mind? Most probably, the universe, the earth, the people, the flashy lights, the weather, your family, and wherever your imagination can go.

Yes!

You are thinking right. But this is the other side of the coin. I want you to dive into the inner world.

What comes to your mind when I say inner world?

Perhaps the stuff we discussed in earlier chapters. Yes! You are right this time, too. But now I want to take your mind eyes on your soul. Just look at it by closing your eyes. Feel it. Go beyond this body and the world you see through your open eyes. Just live it with your honest and true soul for a few seconds.

Do it now!

You see, how rich is your inner world? Did you feel peace? If not, then spend some more time with it. We perceive the outer world same way as we build a connection to our inner world, with our soul.

It suits our life scenario very well. We live in a world where competition is everything now. You can see it everywhere around, in relationships, in career, in money, in status, whatever you can name. And it is not surprising at allthat we disconnected from other people at a soul level.

Competition is healthy until you don't mix your soul with competitive intentions. You know what happens inside us when we do this? We sow a seed of negativity inside us, which as a result grows into a plant of demonic nature. Then what to expect, of course, it will lead us to a peaceless, highly competitive, arrogant, and anxious quality of life.

The outer world is a mirror of our inner world. What we believe inside, we see outside. That's why it is really important to check on you at a soul level. Ask questions to yourself. Feel those answers.

I heard a lot from people that the world nowadays is not good. It is dishonest, cruel, arrogant, brutal, etc. And you are absolutely right! I was too from one of those people. But then I realize, where there is darkness, there is light. If not visibly outside, then it must be inside our hearts as hope.

I know, and I believe that not all people are good-intentioned. But this is also true that not all are bad. And to recognize them, we have a mind along with our heart to differentiate and categorize people as they are.

But if we and other people continue to think like, "all people are not good, we should not do anything good for other people, we must consider everyone as our enemy."

Then tell me, are you benefitting from this thinking? Absolutely not!

You are filling your heart and feeding your mind with negativity.

You can say in your defense, "This is the reality of life. No! It's negativity. You are seeing what your old perceptive mind wants you to see. There are happy and good-intentioned people also livin in this world, who only know how to love, no fake curtains. You have to find them.

But why search on, when you can be one?

Try to connect and communicate with your soul whenever you feel like. You will realize, the outer world is not that as bad as you believe until now. Ask your soul what should we do? Then do whatever your soul feels right. But you have to be honest with your soul.

Trusting your intuition is crucial; the more you lean into it, the stronger it grows. This trust could be a pivotal step in your personal development, helping you navigate the complexities of both your inner world and outer world.

TECHNIQUES TO OVERCOME

Acceptance

Acceptance is the first or most powerful tool we are going to adopt. Because unless we accept our situation, how can we make a way to move forward? Accepting flaws and challenging situations is quite tough, but here the journey to sunshine begins.

Acceptance is not always about accepting things and situations in the external world, with which we are quite or a lot uncomfortable, it is also from inside. Accepting our thoughts, intentions, perceptions, issues, and most importantly, our feelings is a real game.

To make room for new and beautiful things, we have to displace some old things, which are no longer serving us.

Right!

Like this, with the intention of adding harmony in life with love, kindness, excitement, we need to displace old beliefs, thought patterns, and emotional baggage.

Some things are easy to replace and other can be quite tough because we live with those particular things, we are used to feelingthem every day. We are habitual. We have a strong emotional connection with some things.

The same happens to our thoughts and feelings. When we try to form new beliefs and generate happy emotions. Our old neural networks try every possible try to interrupt by playing old past memories of negative circumstances and traumas, rational thinking, and logic.

We unknowingly become addicted to our emotions that we find it very difficult to replace them with good emotions. For example, let's assume that you recently lost a loved one and you are not habitual to living without them for a day. You find yourself very uncomfortable, and you don't want to accept this lose.

Maybe another situation like,

You are a very workaholic person, very much dedicated to your work, and one day, suddenly, you are fired from your job because of any reason, like lay off. Now, you are clueless, what to do with yourself.

Take your time!

Don't rush into the other things just to avoid the consequences of the previous one. Face it. Take yourself step by step. See it as it is. There is a hidden message and a lesson in it. Try to grab that message. You will find that there is good hidden beneath the surface. Accept everything that comes your way.

Here is another thing, accepting things as they are doesn't mean to accept things that feel contradictory to your personal growth. Be mindful. Accept things that are not in our control. Accept things that no longer serve us.

> *Happiness can exist only in acceptance*
>
> **– George Orwell**

Detachment

As the philosophers say, detachment is the path of enlightenment, because when we are no longer attached to people, relations, and even material belongings, we no longer try to control everything. In a sense, we accept it as it is.

Attachment is a beautiful feeling, we all feel with certain people like friends and love, certain relations like family ,and material things like a favorite instrument or a sport. But attached to everything we like and love can be hazardous for our emotional, mental, and physical well-being if not in check.

We, over-sensitive people, don't see things through our eyes; we see this world with our hearts. We like everything that has the potential to make us feel good easily and effortlessly. We get attached. We don't want to lose that feeling at any cost.

We spontaneously become overly possessive and protective of those people and things. It can be anything. You can take examples from your own life. Remember the thing or a relation, you once got attached badly and how did you feel after losing that?

Whenever we become over-possessive and protective, our behavior changes. We disconnect ourselves from other things just to connect with that one thing. A good example can be a love affair, where a person feel good about the other person, try to put every effort to make them feel good, and ignore the rest of the world.

It limits our thinking, feeling, and even social circle. Being too attached to certain people and things is like holding a rope for too long, too tightly with your hands. It can be injurious.

It's good to take care of things and relations, but holding them can make us stuck in one place. That is probably not beneficial for our personal growth.

You may have experienced at least once in your lifetime since now, when your favorite toy in childhood broke and you felt sad or even cried badly for that. Then your parents brought you a new toy and you became happy again. It's easy in childhood to shift focus from one thing to another, because children are flexible in nature.

But in adulthood, it's comparatively tough to let go. We fade the charm of joy by feeling less happy in little things and more sad in unnecessary things. We develop a habit of seeing bad things everywhere, even when we try to find bad in good things too.

So, at this point in life, when we get some people or something materialistic in our lives, which makes us feel good, we become attached. We think that if this is not in my life, I will die!

That's why boundaries are important. A healthy boundary between you and the world, including everything you love. Have you ever paid attention to what religious teachers and monks try to teach us? They say everything is *Maya (illusion);*they have almost nothing in their life, and still live their life in enlightenment. This is the magic of detachment.

Having attachmentsto a lot of things in life will only make us feel emotionally drained at regular periods, because in life,nothing is permanent in this planetary world.

I am not advising you to become a cold-hearted person. But becoming a little selfish with your emotions has no side effects. Try to keep everything in balance, including your emotions. Because the less you will attached, the more you will open yourself to experience the world that your eyes can see and the soul you can feel. It will help you to grow as a person.

The more you grow, the more enlightened you will feel. You will be at peace when things will not bother you because fear of losing attached people and attachment is the only fear we live in.

By detaching ourselves, by making healthy boundaries, we can enhance our emotional balance, outer relations with people,and closeness to materialistic things.

So, make healthy boundaries, free yourself from fear of attachment, and open your heart to widen your horizon. Give more love and life without getting stuck in the cage of attachment.

Detachment is an art of enjoying something while always being open to the possibility of losing it someday

– John B. Bejo

Journaling

Journaling is really a good and enjoyable technique you can perform. Maybe you are already familiar with the term and already applying it. But if not, here we go! In both cases, I want to explain journaling in my own words.

Journaling is a release of thoughts and visuals from our mind to the page directly. Not blockage. This feels like a stress buster because when we write something that we cannot say easily from our lips, it releases the unspoken emotions of things. It can be related to anything.

It helped me a lot during my phase. I was not a diary writer kind of girl. But I had a diary at my desk with my other books. I used to see it daily and used to ignore it daily. But one day, all of a sudden, I decided to write something about that day. So, I wrote whatever my mind was chattering about. And from the point I wrote the first alphabet to the full stop at last. It was a whole journey of emotions between these two points I never knew existed inside me. I felt so relaxed, like I released all my unspoken words and energies onto the paper. It was like therapy. From that day, I started to write journals in my diary regularly.

If you already do journals, try to write more deeply. And if you are new to this. Relax! You can start from scratch. Start from the current day. Write about your day, the best thing about your day, the worst thing about your day, the people you meet, the things you do and enjoy, and how all these things made you feel. Write whatever your mind filled is with; just release it onto the paper.

Do journal... Write your unspoken words here.

What do you have in your mind right now?

Benefits of journaling:

- ***Self-discovery:***Journaling encourages reflection and insights about your thoughts, feelings, and desires. It can help you uncover patterns in your behavior and beliefs. You will get a clear idea of what your mind says and how.
- ***Emotional release:***Writing about your emotions allows for a healthy release of unspoken feelings. It will help you to release stress and anxiety. It creates a safe space to explore complex emotions without judgment.
- ***Clarity and problem solving:***Putting your thoughts on paper can bring mental clarity to confusing situations. It provides a roadmap or structured way to analyze problems and brainstorm potential solutions.
- ***Increased mindfulness:***Engaging in regular journaling fosters mindfulness by encouraging you to slow down and reflect on your daily experiences and emotions.
- ***Better communication skills:***Writing regularly can enhance your ability to articulate thoughts and feelings. This practice helps to improve written and verbal communication over time.

These are a few benefits that you will experience with your writing. Even medical practitioner suggests using this practice as a therapy. Psychologist and psychiatrist advise their patients to write deep, unspoken things that cause inner turbulence, that they are not comfortable telling anyone. But apart from medical science, we can do it in our daily life, not just to release stress but also to keep a track record of our emotional journey.

Little Moments

In a world full of flashy lights, we often neglect the little things of joy that fill the gaps of our daily life in beautiful ways. We tend to forget the moments in this big, tense world.

Ever noticed children? They are full of life. Enjoy every little thing. They put themselves completely into the things to enjoy the most. But when these children grow big like you and me, they change their priorities for happiness and enjoyment. Now, they have bigger life goals, bigger targets to achieve, bigger positions to promote at work, bigger bank balance to make, and among all these things, we forget the most important thing to achieve – happiness!

Just take a look things above. Don't we do all these things to make ourselves happy? In fact, whatever we do in our lives, the end goal is to make ourselves happy. Right! But as our age increases, we reduce the number of moments to be happy. We make a concise list of limited things in our life and think that only this can make me happy, like getting a job, getting married, having children, perfect vacations, and anything you want to add.

No!

You already have a lot in your life to be happy and grateful for, right now. Our feelings are not limited to certain situations where we can feel happiness. It is infinite. You can feel happiness in anything you can make your mind to.

Look around yourself, and you will find hundreds of things to be grateful for. Don't ignore even the smallest thing. It contributes too. Think about your family and friends, your favorite outfit, loved ones, the weather, your good health, the money you have already, those happy moments you spent well in your life, your house, your room, the chair you sit on, this book, and a lot more.

See, how many reasons you already have to feel grateful for. How blessed you are already.

Focusing on the lack:

We humans have a tendency to focus most of the time on things we don't have or wish to have, and in order to dream about those things, we forget about the things we already have. We miss the moment of wealth by focusing on lack.

If we cannot be grateful for the things we already have, and things we once wished to have them and now it is available to us. Then how can we feel happiness for the things we will have in the future?

I read somewhere, people who are less destined than us, are leading a more emotionally fulfilling lives than us. But how? How can someone be happy if he has nothing to be happy for?

I used to ask the same question before. Then I found out the formula for their happiness.

Accept + Gratitude

=

Happiness and

Peace

They develop the ability to accept the things they have no control over. They accept things they can't change and appreciate the things they have.

A friend of mine is always insecure about his financial situation. Although he is from a good financial background. But still, he wants a lot of money and materialistic things, and always talks about only this. One day, he met with an accident. He was in the ICU for about a month, and now he is grateful for every single breath.

As we talked earlier, we only care about the things when we can no longer have them in our lives. But if you have something you can feel grateful for. Just appreciate it. Not everyone has everything.

Take a task and be grateful for as many things as you can. You can write them too in your journal. Make a long list. And whenever you feel sad, just open that list and see what you have.

Things I am grateful for

You can start like this

I am grateful for my…..

Go close to nature

Do you know? People who live in villages or less urban cities are happier than those people live in big metro cities. The reason behind it is that people living in village are closer to nature as compared to people living in urban areas.

That's why people living in urban areas are more likely to spend their vacations in nature, like green mountains, beaches, ponds, rivers, waterfall, snow, etc. And people living in villages find it difficult to adjust in urban areas as compared to urban people in villages.

Relax! We don't need to shift our house in a village. All we have to do is steal time from our routine urban life to spend in nature.

The benefits of spending some moments in nature are numerous. Some are here:

- ***Stress reduction:*** Immersing oneself in natural surroundings lowers cortisol levels, effectively reducing stress and promoting relaxation.
- ***Improved mood:***Exposure to nature helps in improving mood, leads to enhancement of mood, and reduces symptoms of anxiety and depression.
- ***Increment in mindfulness:***Nature encourages mindfulness by prompting us to be present in the moment. Paying attention to natural details like the sound of leaves, exposure to sunlight, wide sky, and warmth of the sun enhances awareness and reduces distractions.
- ***Feeling of oneness:*** spending time in nature leads us to feel oneness with nature, causing us to release negative thoughts and emotions.
- ***Wholeness:*** feelings of wholeness overwhelm us when we come close to nature. Give us positivity and recharge our energy.

There are many other benefits too of getting close to nature. The color of leaves, trees, chilling under their shadows, the fragrance of flowers, gives relaxation to the body senses and enhances mood. Releasing a lot of happy hormones like dopamine and sleep hormones like serotonin helps us reduce distress and good sleep.

You know why we feel this much relaxation and fulfillment in nature, because we are a part of nature. We are nature. We are not a separate being from nature. Our whole life depends on nature. Even our life cycle is an amazing process of nature. Our emotions, our true nature, true behavior, and true thoughts all come from nature itself.

Nature is a mirror of oneself, our human experience, emotions, changes, and growth. Changing seasons describe our emotional well-being very well, like the changing of seasons from the shedding of leaves to the beauty of greenery, from the heat of summer to the coolness of winter. Nature reflects with joy.

We can perform various activities in nature to relax our minds from negative thoughts and emotions. Here is where you can perform:

- Planting seedlings
- Walk in a garden
- Talking to trees
- Cycling
- Hiking
- Smelling fragrance of flowers

- Looking at the sky
- Star gazing

Add yours here

How do you connect with nature?

All the world is a stage. And all men and women merely players

– William Shakespeare

Be creative

Creativity is a spiritual essence. Few know how it tastes and others just neglect. But I am calling this 'spiritual'? Because when we do what we truly want to do, we connect to our spirit. As I mentioned, our soul knows everything.

All the geniuses of all time, whoever you can remember, Albert Einstein, Leonardo Da Vinci, Thomas Alva Edison, Plato, Aristotle, Picasso, Galileo, all had one common thing in their life. Do you know what that is? Suffering from pain and loneliness. If you research, you will find it's true.

Every art and invention these creative geniuses made was the way to express and release their innermost feelings and emotions. They all find their own unique way to open themselves.

Leonardo expressed in his paintings, Mozart expressed in his symphonies, philosophers like Socrates, Plato and Aristotle in their writings, and other great minds in their own art.

You may have thoughts in your mind like, they are geniuses, their intelligence is remarkable, they were brilliant, but I am not. I am not creative. I did nothing creative in my whole life; I cannot do this. I cannot be like them. Now, tell me, who is asking you to be like them? Be you! Be yourself! You don't need to try to copy anyone to perfection. Take inspiration from your ideals. Study them. Know them. Acknowledge them. Appreciate them.

If you already know where your heart flows, it's good. Go for it! But if you are yet to struggle in this aspect, try everything your heart desires. There are numerous activities this world has to offer us, like music, art, painting, writing, singing, cooking, dancing, literature, etc, anything you want. You don't need to excel at everything. Just try your hand at as much as activities you can, and pick one or two that suit you the most. And if you have diverse interests, go for all, shift from one to another.

The other thing that is most common among the above geniuses is their passion and dedication towards their interest. They dare themselves to look like a fool in this judgmental world and showed their uniqueness to the world and became remarkable.

You may be a working professional, a student, a housewife, steals some time from your exhausting routine and fills yourself up with spirituality and enlightenment by releasing your in-depth emotions through your creativity and showing your uniqueness.

You may think thatyou don't have the resources to improve your creative endeavours. But you don't need a proper studio of yourself where you can do everything in privacy, start from scratch! Just start! You don't have to see the final destination. Fill yourself up with courage and start.

Enjoy yourself in your '*me time*' along with improving yourself. That is also an achievement. Take your creativity to the next level. See, where your heart beats the most. This is like a calling from the soul to put your heart into creativity. Enjoy new experiences. Take rides in your emotional roller coaster.

Here are some benefits of being creative:

- Makes your mind sharp and open
- Releases emotions

- Heightened sensual feelings
- Sense of liveliness
- An originality of yours in the world
- Your legacy

Write about your creative journey in your journal and track a record of your feelings and emotions. Look at the improvement you made. Celebrate them!

Recreate joy

When I was in my climax of depressing phase, I was regretting that I did nothing in my golden period of my life, where I could actually enjoy a lot. How much time did I waste being depressed? I was sad. I was complaining about my precious time I lost. Then one day, a thought randomly clicked into my mind that, "ok! I lost a lot of time, but I am continuing to losing it in complaining. I learnt my lessons then, why take this so far anymore? I need to stop regretting from now on and must live my life. "

Then I decided to leave the past and go on with the present towards a happy future. I made a list of things I denied doing or learning in my depressing phase and began to add them to my life slowly. The present I was living would soon be my future, and I was regretting my past, and I don't want to think the same in my future for this present. And it immediately filled my body with extreme energy. I began to organize my mental life, aligning with my outer life.

I know, this is not possible to fill the gaps of past; it can't be reversed. But we can fill happy moments in our present. We can create happiness as much as we want. All we have is our present now. Whatever happened, happened! It's no longer serving us. So, there is no need to hold its branches anymore. It's time to recreate life from scratch. Right now! Right here!

Think about the things you can do right now that make you happy. Think about the resources you already have that give you a sense of meaning. We already wasted a lot of time in feeding negative emotions. So, it's time to live double. It's time to receive happiness with interest.

Fill every moment of your life with positive and lively feelings/ every second with hope and optimism. This is the only way to live with our full potential.

But now you know that no complaint, no blame, no request, no begging can help you. Only you can help yourself, and you should. Only you know where you are at your emotional level, what is running in your mind, what perceptions your mind's eye made, only you know.

And here is another thing, no one also knows what makes you happy at peak, what you love most, what desires you have in the corner of your heart, no one knows, because everyone is living individually in this human body.

Whether we know it or not, accept it or not, but ahead of this world, our society, our family and friends, spouse and children, there is a world of individuality, where we know where we live completely in our individual form. There is nothing right or wrong, there is nothing good or bad, there is nothing true or false, there is everything is our own, personal. Only you know about that world, where you fully expose yourself, who you truly are. And every person keeps this kind of their unique world in their mind.

So, in your world, what do you like? What is your favorite thing to do in your spare time? What do you think about other people? Are your thoughts healthy? Do you like to explore? Do you like to work with people? What charges you up- travelling or book reading?

Whatever you like, fill your life with those rejuvenating things and activities. You have to take charge of your happy life. Do whatever your heart feels good about.

How can you recreate your life?

Self-love

I am sure you are not unfamiliar with the term "self-love". You may often hear this term people saying, "self-love is important." But what is the exact meaning of self-love? How can one love himself or herself?

Good question!

In a similar way, how do we express love to the other person? Think about it! How do we take care of other person when we are in love with them? We care for most little things that can make them happy or sad as well. We put in efforts. We take care of their feelings. We show respect. We listen to them. We care for our image they have in their mind. We love to talk to them. We try to provide everything they want. Right! This is the way we express our love to other people.

Why always other people, why not us? Why don't we put effort to make ourselves happy? Why don't we care of our feelings and only care about the other's feelings? Because we may think that taking care of ourselves and our own feelings is an act of selfishness. We may develop feelings of guilt and shame.

No wonder!

Because our society is running on the philosophy of making other people happy. They believe that one should take care of another, and this is absolutely right! But making other people happy by sacrificing our own happiness is just not fair.

They don't understand this little thing that when a person himself will happy, everybody will come into the aura of that happiness. When a person himself is happy, he does good deeds, tries to spread only happiness everywhere.

Applicable to other feelings too, for example – anger. When a single person in a group shows anger, everybody else also comes into the aura of aggression and feelsthe same feelings.

Making oneself happy is not a sin. It's a prayer. Every single human being on this earth deserves to be happy and he/she should not expect this happiness, and love from outside. It all starts from within. When you love yourself, only then you can love other people. And showing oneself love with little effort is all justified.

Go for it!

But how can we express this love with ourselves?

- ***Accept your flaws:***There is not a single human being on earth who is perfect. Everybody has got their own flaws. No one is untouched by flaws; you have yours, I have mine. All we can do is accept and embrace. That's it!
- ***Take care:***Take care of yourself in terms of mental, emotional, and physical well-being. Three of these are important. For mental well-being, you can do meditation, journaling, etc. For emotional well-being, you can enjoy your favorite hobby. For physical, do exercise, yoga, and walking.
- ***Appreciation:***Appreciate yourself for little achievements. It may happen that other people do not feelas much excitement as you do and give importance to your little achievements that matter to you in your heart. But it's ok! You celebrate.
- ***Go alone:***Go for a movie, go for a coffee date, and go for a dinner date with yourself. Embrace your

individuality. Spend quality time with yourself. Be confident in your own skin.

These are a few, but you can add more things that you would like to show love with yourself.

Write here….

Present moment

The present moment is the only moment we live in. Everything else is just imagination, whether it is of the past or the future. And you know what, where the problem lies? When we get to realize that in most of our present time, we only think about the past or future. The things that already happened and about the things that can happen in the future.

We don't lose only our present moment, but also fill our minds with destructive and aimless thinking. Think about it! But what does it mean to be fully present? It means to put your whole attention only on the present moment.

For example, if you are reading this book, are you putting your whole attention to every single word or are you imagining something else between the words? There is a heavy possibility that you are. Did you get my point?

It's easy to control our thoughts, because we are used to including everything relevant to irrelevant in our mind, and are unable to eliminate them whenever we want.

In this case, we are not using our mind; our mind is using us. Think about it! Can you stop thinking whenever you want? Yes! Maybe for a few seconds, but then your mind again will take over you with thoughts. Maybe you are questioning what it means to stop thinking? How can one? And why should one?

Because the essence of living can only be known in the present moment. Stopping thinking is like an 'off' button of the mind. As we know that our mind is like an electrical tool. So, like other tools, it also needs rest and off time. We need to learn its 'off' and 'on' system.

But how?

By being fully present in the present moment. By paying more attention to the activities you do in the present and if not doing anything or just lying on the bed, then too live the present moment. With the 'off' button, I am referring to living in the eternal present, and with the 'on', I am referring to the relational thinking we need to do for our future.

But again, as I already mentioned, it is not possible to know about the future events for the whole life. We don't know what will happen next. We only need to plan our next two steps in the right direction, as our heart guides us.

Think like this! You are driving a car from A city to B city in the dark night, where you are not able to see anything but darkness, and the headlights of your car can show you the next hundred meters ahead. Can you drive? Of course, you can.

As similar to this, we don't need to be tense about our whole life. We just need to move consistently while living our present and keep an eye on our next two steps. And these two steps will take you wherever you want to go.

Trust them!

I read a lot of self-help books, and one common practice I found was 'meditation'. We all know what meditation is. But what meditation is for? What mediation practices try to teach us? As per my understanding, meditation simply teaches us to be in the present moment by focusing on our breathing. Isn't it?

If you have time, then you can perform this activity by staying still in one place. But, if you don't have a lot of time, no worries! You can meditate at any moment you want. All you have to do is focus your mind on the present.

Only the present moment has the power to vanish unwanted thoughts of the past and the future. Being simply in the present creates the essence of oneness in this world. Being in "human being" points towards the present moment to live in a 'being' state. It can take some time to learn to live in a totally present state, but it will be all worthful. Train your mind to be in the present from now!

You are not alone

You may often think that you are the only one who is suffering from adisease like depression, and anxiety and makes it a personal pain to suffer alone. We begin to suffer in silence and refuse to tell anyone for reasons like, “maybe they will not understand”. You don’t want this case because it will only increase the pain inside you. Right!

But let me know you, you are not the only one who thinks like this, almost everyone, at least in one phase of life, thinks the same. Your pain is not your personal pain.

It is the collective truth of life that we share in a human form. You are not separate.

But there is a chance of possibility that you may isolate yourself in a closed door and refuse to see the pain of others. Others are feeling the same. Maybe they are feeling right now, or maybe they are going to.

Being depressed and sad is not a thing to feel guilty or ashamed of. Maybe depression in the bigger picture is perceived as a cave of darkness. But the precious and worthy things are foundin mines. Right!

Depression is not a punishment, it's a signal to introspect your inner being, feel your individuality, see life in a different way, learn from it, move from it, and live life to its full potential.

I don't know what stage you are in, but I do know is now is the time to free yourself from the cage of darkness. You are meant to be happy. You deserve to be happy. You are destined to live your life to the fullest in this birth.

Don't hold yourself anymore. Whatever we do is to make ourselves happy only. The only motive to live is to be happy for whatever reason you want. We live in the hope of being happy. Don't wait to find happiness in outer things.

Don't expect happiness from other people; create your happiness. Do whatever makes you happy without relying on anyone. To make you happy is not anyone else's responsibility. They have their task to make themselves happy.

Fill yourself up with love. Love gives energy,assadness reduces energy. Be energetic in the aura of love. Love everything you have in your life. Love the little moments you like in your daily life. Record them. Embrace them. Collect the happy moments from memories.

Being happy is not that hard. We just need to make a decision to be happy no matter what and to be consistent with the decision. No one else can make this decision for you. It's completely your personal choice to live in a happy life or to remain in a depressed life.

Don't let your mind interrupt decision, because it loves to be in the comfort zone of one state, whether it is sadness or happiness. Then why the sadness? Convert it to be in a happy state. Change your neural network.

Try to be happy in as manynlittle things as possible. Make yourself like a child to when you have nothing to be tense about, and enjoy the little pleasures of life.

Show your maturity when it is needed. Don't take the burden of maturity every single time. Don't let your maturity ruin the childishness of your inner child.

Live life at the
level you never
lived before

Author's Bio

Vishakha Soni is a debut author in the self-help genre, dedicated to guiding readers toward clarity and purpose. Through personal experience and practical wisdom, she empower individuals to live more authentically and find joy amidst life's challenges. Her first book, Joy Above Mental Clouds: A Practical Guide To Clarity, Peace And Purpose, is a testament to the belief that true well-being is within everyone's reach.